SOME IMPORTANT PLACES IN GEORGIA O'KEEFFE'S LIFE

1. **Sun Prairie, Wisconsin**. Georgia was born on her family's dairy farm near here in 1887.

2. **Virginia**. The O'Keeffe family moved to Williamsburg, Virginia, in 1902. Georgia finished high school there and attended art classes at the University of Virginia.

3. **New York, New York**. During Georgia's time, New York City was becoming a center of modern art. As a young woman, Georgia spent a year studying at the Art Students League there. Later she would move back to New York and create amazing flower and city scene paintings.

4. **Amarillo and Canyon, Texas**. Georgia taught art classes in both Amarillo and Canyon. It was here that she became inspired by the vastness of the land and began some of her first abstract works.

5. **Santa Fe, Taos, and Abiquiu, New Mexico**. When Georgia first visited Santa Fe in 1917, she fell in love with the awesome natural beauty of the desert and mountains. She returned to New Mexico often to paint scenes. Eventually she bought a house near Abiquiu, New Mexico.

THIS IS THE AREA THAT'S SHOWN ON THE LARGER MAP

TIMELINE OF GEORGIA O'KEEFFE'S LIFE

1887 Georgia O'Keeffe is born in Sun Prairie, Wisconsin.

1899 Georgia takes art lessons at home. She decides to become an artist when she grows up.

1902 The O'Keeffe family moves to Williamsburg, Virginia.

1905 Georgia studies at the Art Institute of Chicago.

1908 Georgia attends the Art Students League in New York City.

1912 Georgia studies at the University of Virginia. She then moves to Amarillo, Texas, to be a teacher in the public schools.

1916 Alfred Stieglitz, a New York photographer and art gallery owner, sees some of Georgia's abstract charcoal drawings, and displays them at his gallery.

1917 Georgia visits New Mexico for the first time. She is crazy about the scenery there.

THIS WAY

UP HERE

1918 Encouraged by Alfred Stieglitz, Georgia moves to New York City to become a full-time artist. Over the next few years, she and Alfred fall in love.

1924 Georgia and Alfred marry. Georgia begins her large flower paintings.

1929 Georgia goes to New Mexico and begins painting remarkable desert scenes.

1945 Georgia buys an adobe house outside Abiquiu, New Mexico.

1946 Alfred Stieglitz dies in New York City at the age of 82.

1949 Georgia O'Keeffe moves permanently to New Mexico.

1950 Georgia travels all over the world.

1971 Georgia begins to have eye problems. She starts doing fewer paintings.

1973 Georgia works on a book and video about her life.

1986 Georgia O'Keeffe dies in Santa Fe at the age of 98.

GETTING TO KNOW THE WORLD'S GREATEST ARTISTS

GEORGIA
O'KEEFFE

WRITTEN AND ILLUSTRATED BY MIKE VENEZIA

CONSULTANT MEG MOSS

CHILDREN'S PRESS®

An Imprint of Scholastic Inc.

New York Toronto London Auckland Sydney
Mexico City New Delhi Hong Kong
Danbury, Connecticut

For my very original daughter, Elizabeth

Cover: *Pelvis II*. 1944. Oil on canvas, 40 x 30 in. (101.6 x 76.2 cm).
© The Metropolitan Museum of Art, George A. Hearn Fund. Image
source: Art Resource, NY.

Work by Georgia O'Keeffe: © 2014 Georgia O'Keeffe Museum/
Artists Rights Society (ARS), New York

Library of Congress Cataloging-in-Publication Data

Venezia, Mike, author, illustrator.
  Georgia O'Keeffe / written and illustrated by Mike Venezia. –
Revised edition.
      pages cm. – (Getting to know the world's greatest artists)
  Summary: "Introduces the reader to the artist Georgia O'Keeffe"–
Provided by publisher.
  Audience: 8-9.
  Includes bibliographical references and index.
  ISBN 978-0-531-21314-8 (library binding : alk. paper) – ISBN
978-0-531-21291-2 (pbk. : alk. paper) 1. O'Keeffe, Georgia,
1887-1986–Juvenile literature. 2. Painters–United
States–Biography–Juvenile literature. 3. Women painters–United
States–Biography–Juvenile literature. I. Title. II. Series: Venezia,
Mike. Getting to know the world's greatest artists.

  ND237.O5V46 2015
  759.13–dc23
  [B]   2014042743

13 14 15 R 25 24 23

Scholastic Inc. 557 Broadway, New York 10012

Georgia O'Keeffe: A Portrait, by Alfred Stieglitz 1918.
Gelatin silver print, 3 ½ x 4 ½ inches.
National Gallery of Art, Washington, Alfred Stieglitz Collection.

Georgia O'Keeffe was born on her family's large Wisconsin farm in 1887. She would grow up to become one of America's most famous painters. Her clear, bright paintings show the beauty she found in the simple, natural things around her.

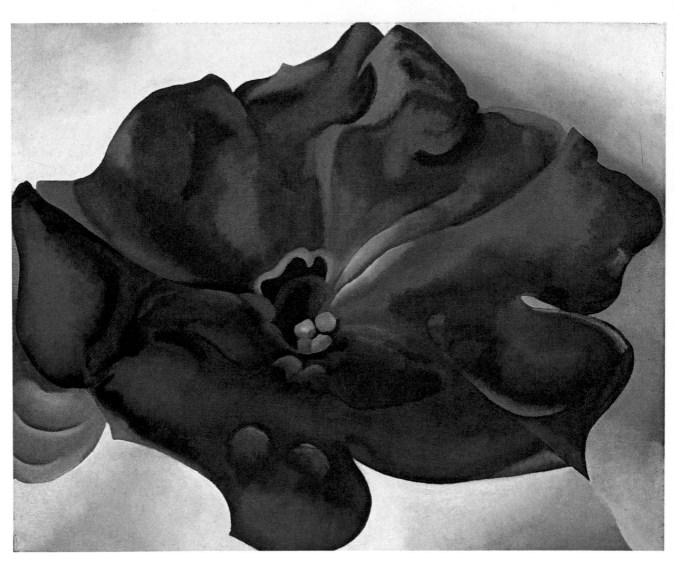

Petunia, by Georgia O'Keeffe. 1925. Oil on canvas,
18 x 22 inches. The Farber Collection, New York.

Georgia loved to paint flowers,
mountains, seashells, and even
animal bones she found in the desert.

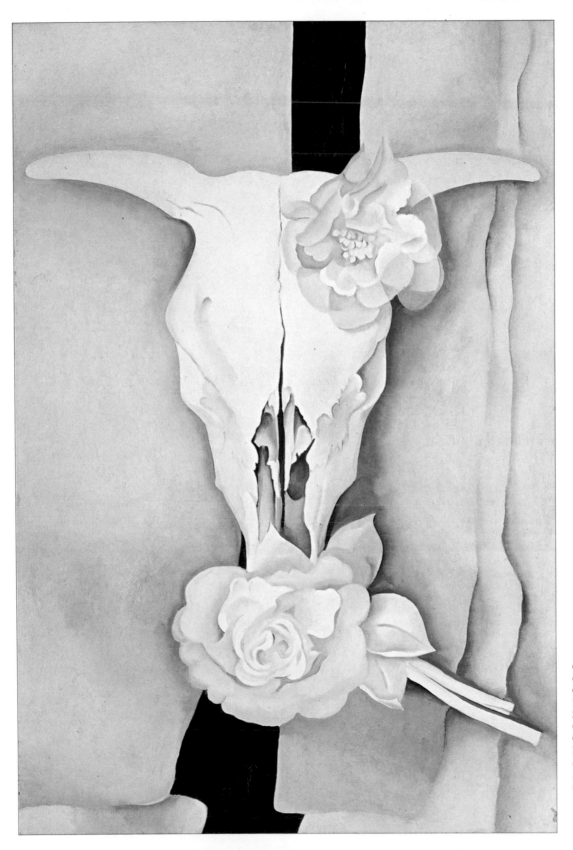

Cow's Skull with Calico Roses, by Georgia O'Keeffe. 1931. Oil on canvas, $35^9/_{10}$ x 24 inches. Gift of Georgia O'Keeffe, 1947.712. Photograph courtesy of The Art Institute of Chicago.

5

Sky Above Clouds IV, by Georgia O'Keeffe. 1965.
Oil on canvas, 96 x 288 inches.
Restricted gift of the Paul and Gabriella Rosenbaum Foundation,
gift of Georgia O'Keeffe, 1983.821.
Photograph © 1993, The Art Institute of Chicago.
All Rights Reserved.

Even though Georgia was interested in all kinds of natural

things, she hardly ever painted
pictures of people or animals.

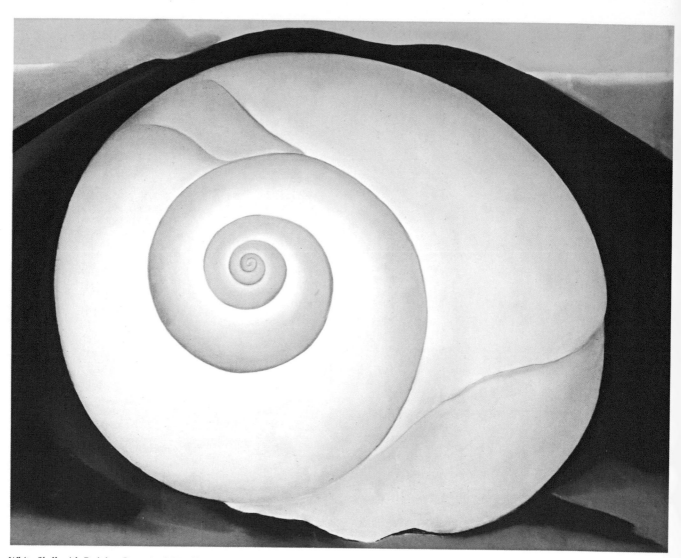

White Shell with Red, by Georgia O'Keeffe. 1938. Pastel on paper, 21 x 27 inches.
Alfred Stieglitz Collection, bequest of Georgia O'Keeffe, 1987.250.5.
Photograph courtesy of The Art Institute of Chicago.

Georgia often rearranged the
natural things she saw, and simplified
them. She made the seashell above
very large, to give it a special power
and strength.

Blue and Green Music, by Georgia O'Keeffe. 1919. Oil on canvas, 23 x 19 inches.
Alfred Stieglitz Collection, gift of Georgia O'Keeffe, 1969.835.
Photograph © 1992, The Art Institute of Chicago. All Rights Reserved.

Sometimes she painted shapes
and colors that she saw in her mind.

The farm where Georgia grew up
was a great place to learn about
nature. Georgia wanted to touch and
feel everything she could get her
hands on.

Georgia remembered that when
she was very little, she put dirt in her
mouth to see what it tasted like!

Georgia's mother thought art was very important, and made sure Georgia and her sisters had art lessons while they were growing up. Georgia did so well with her lessons that her parents encouraged her to go to art college after she graduated from high school. Georgia studied at different art schools and colleges all over the country.

Dead Rabbit with Copper Pot, by Georgia O'Keeffe. 1908.
Oil on canvas, 19 x 23 ½ inches.
Art Students League, New York. Photograph by Dave Forbert.

At one school, in New York City,
she won a prize for her painting of
a rabbit and copper pot.

Georgia liked New York City. It was busier and more exciting than the peaceful farm areas where she had grown up. Georgia often visited a small gallery in New York that showed the work of new artists. It was owned by a well-known photographer named Alfred Stieglitz.

Alfred loved modern art and tried to get people interested in modern European artists, like Paul Cezanne

Above: *The Large Bathers*, by Paul Cezanne. 1906. Oil on canvas, 82 x 99 inches. Philadelphia Museum of Art, purchased, W.P. Wilstach Collection.

Below: *The Red Studio*, by Henri Matisse. 1911. Oil on canvas, 71¼ x 86¼ inches. The Museum of Modern Art, New York, Mrs. Simon Guggenheim Fund. Photograph © 1993, The Museum of Modern Art, New York.

and Henri Matisse, and American artists, like John Marin and Marsden Hartley.

Georgia didn't know it at the time, but in a few years, Alfred would help get people interested in her paintings, too.

Above: *Painting No. 48*, by Marsden Hartley. 1913. Oil on canvas, 47 ³⁄₁₆ x 47 ³⁄₁₆ inches. The Brooklyn Museum, Dick S. Ramsay Fund.

After finishing school, Georgia decided to teach art for a while, and traveled to Texas to take a job there. She found it an exciting place to be. Georgia loved the clear skies and the hot, bright sun. She felt the energy and power of the dust storms and heat lightning she saw at night.

Evening Star, No. V, by Georgia O'Keeffe. 1917.
Watercolor, 8 5/8 x 11 5/8 inches. Marion Koogler McNay Art Museum,
San Antonio, Texas, Bequest of Helen Miller Jones.

Georgia started to show the
excitement she felt about Texas in her
paintings. Soon her work looked
different from the work of any other
artist.

During this time, Alfred Stieglitz
became very interested in Georgia

O'Keeffe. He remembered her from her visits to his gallery, and had seen some of her newest works of art. Alfred thought Georgia could become one of the best American artists ever.

Alfred wrote a letter to Georgia and asked her to come back to New York. He told her he could raise enough money so she wouldn't have to work and could spend all her time painting. He also offered to show her artwork in his gallery.

Georgia found it hard to leave the beauty of Texas, but decided Alfred's offer was too good to miss out on.

After she arrived in New York, Georgia began painting bold shapes

Red Canna, by Georgia O'Keeffe. c. 1923. Oil on canvas, 36 x 29 ⅞ inches. Collection of The University of Arizona Museum, Tucson, Gift of Oliver James.

and designs, covering her canvases with bright color. Soon her work changed, and she began painting the beautiful flowers that helped to make her famous.

Morning Glory with Black, by Georgia O'Keeffe. c. 1926. Oil on canvas, 35 13/16 x 39 5/8 inches. The Cleveland Museum of Art, Bequest of Leonard C. Hanna, Jr., 58.42.

Georgia usually made her flowers very large. She hoped they would make people feel the same wonderful way she felt when she looked at real flowers. Georgia thought her large

flowers might even get busy New Yorkers to stop and notice them.

Georgia's paintings got attention right away. At first, people were curious to see the work of a woman artist. In the 1920s, there weren't many well-known women artists. It didn't take long for people to realize that Georgia O'Keeffe wasn't just a woman artist. She was a great American artist!

Even though Georgia needed
money to live, she felt funny about
selling her art. Georgia worked hard
on her paintings, and felt so close to
them that she hated to see them leave
the gallery. They were almost like her
children.

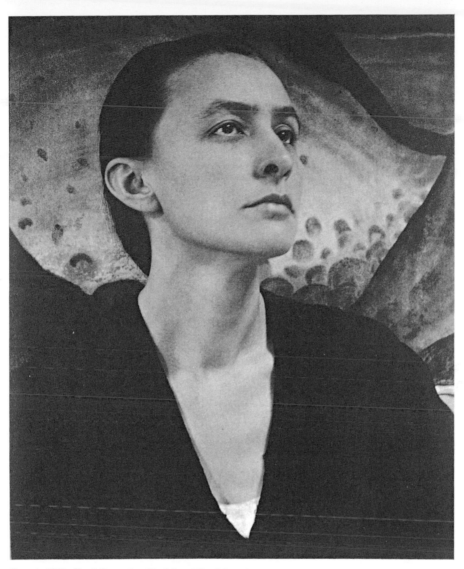

Georgia O'Keeffe: A Portrait—Head, by Alfred Stieglitz. 1918.
Palladium print, toned with gold, 9 ½ x 7 ⅝ inches.
National Gallery of Art, Washington, Alfred Stieglitz Collection.

In between painting and showing her work, Georgia agreed to model for Alfred Stieglitz. Alfred thought Georgia was very beautiful and took many famous photographs of her.

East River from the 30th Story of the Shelton Hotel,
by Georgia O'Keeffe. 1928. Oil on canvas, 30 x 48 inches.
From the collection of the New Britain Museum of American Art,
Connecticut, Stephen Lawrence Fund. Photograph by E. Irving Blomstrann.

Alfred and Georgia had respected each other's talent for a long time. Now that Georgia was living in New York and working closely with Alfred, they found themselves falling in love. In 1924, they decided to get married.

They moved into an apartment high up in a big hotel. Georgia loved the wide-open view she saw, and started painting pictures of the city. This surprised people, because in the 1920s, powerful city scenes were usually done only by men.

New York, Night, by Georgia O'Keeffe. 1928-29. Oil on canvas, 40 1/8 x 19 1/8 inches. Sheldon Memorial Art Gallery, University of Nebraska-Lincoln, Nebraska Art Association-Thomas C. Woods Memorial Collection.

25

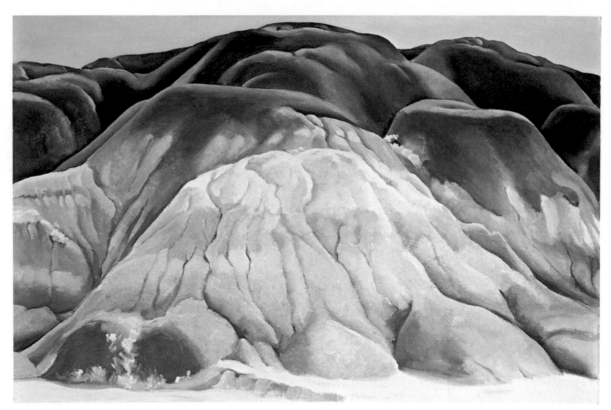

Grey Hills, by Georgia O'Keeffe. 1942.
Oil on canvas, 20 x 30 inches. © 1993 Indianapolis Museum of Art,
Gift of Mr. and Mrs. James W. Fesler.

Several years later, Georgia was
invited out West to visit some friends
in New Mexico. She thought the desert
and clear blue skies there were even
more exciting than the scenery in Texas.
Georgia began painting the animal
bones, desert flowers, and sun-baked
adobe churches she found there.

Georgia especially loved the
mountains in New Mexico. They
seemed almost alive to her. In some
paintings, you might get the feeling
that Georgia's mountains could get
up and move around.

Ranchos Church, by Georgia O'Keeffe.
c. 1930. Oil on canvas, 24 x 36 inches.
The Phillips Collection, Washington, D.C.

Georgia spent most of the rest
of her life painting in New Mexico.
Alfred agreed it was the best place
for her to be in order to make her
paintings as good as possible.

Georgia only traveled back to New York for a few months every year to be with Alfred and show her work. Years later, after Alfred died, Georgia moved to New Mexico for good.

Georgia O'Keeffe lived to be 98 years old. She decided to become an artist at a time when it was proper only for women to teach art.

Georgia didn't care what people thought about her, or her art. She worked hard on her paintings and put her own special feeling into them.

Black Cross, New Mexico, by Georgia O'Keeffe. 1929.
Oil on canvas, 39 x 30 inches.
Art Institute Purchase Fund, 1943.95.
Photograph courtesy of The Art Institute of Chicago.

Georgia met many famous artists during her life. She learned a lot from them, but never copied their styles or joined their groups.

Pelvis with the Distance, by Georgia O'Keeffe. 1943.
Oil on canvas, 23⅞ x 29¾ inches.
© Indianapolis Museum of Art, Gift of Anne Marmon Greenleaf in memory of Carolyn Marmon Fesler.

Pattern of Leaves, by Georgia O'Keeffe. 1924.
Oil on canvas, 22⅛ x 18⅛ inches.
The Phillips Collection, Washington, D.C.

Because of this, Georgia O'Keeffe's paintings are very original. She often found beauty in things that most people would ignore or never even notice, and was able to show that beauty in her paintings.

If you get a chance to see a real Georgia O'Keeffe painting, you'll probably notice how bright and clear the colors are. This is because Georgia paid special attention to her painting materials. She always bought the best brushes and paint, no matter how much they cost her.

The paintings in this book come from the museums listed below.

The Art Institute of Chicago, Chicago, Illinois
The Brooklyn Museum, Brooklyn, New York
The Cleveland Museum of Art, Cleveland, Ohio
Indianapolis Museum of Art, Indianapolis, Indiana
The Metropolitan Museum of Art, New York, New York
The Museum of Modern Art, New York, New York
Marion Koogler McNay Art Museum, San Antonio, Texas
National Gallery of Art, Washington, D.C.
New Britain Museum of American Art, New Britain, Connecticut
Philadelphia Museum of Art, Philadelphia, Pennsylvania
The Phillips Collection, Washington, D.C.
Sheldon Memorial Art Gallery, Lincoln, Nebraska
The University of Arizona Museum, Tucson, Arizona

LEARN MORE BY TAKING THE O'KEEFFE QUIZ!

(ANSWERS ON THE NEXT PAGE.)

1. Why did Georgia collect animal bones from the desert and bring them back to her home in New York?
- a She wanted to sell them to soup companies to make some extra money.
- b She wanted them as treats for her pet dog.
- c She wanted to use them as models for her still-life paintings.

2. Georgia loved music as much as art. What instruments did she play?
- a Violin
- b Conga drums
- c Piano

3. What were Georgia's favorite pets?
- a Miniature coyotes
- b Chow dogs
- c Cats
- d Gila monsters

4. What were Georgia's favorite fashion styles and colors?
- a Gold-sequined pants suits
- b Spandex running gear
- c Plain black dresses with simple white blouses

5. Georgia's largest painting, *Sky Above Clouds IV*, was too big to fit in her studio, so she decided to paint it in her garage. What was her biggest worry while painting it?
- a That an 8 x 24-foot painting would be too large to fit through any art museum door when it was completed.
- b That someone might try parking their car in the garage, and run over the painting.
- c That a rattlesnake or two might slither in the garage while she was painting.

ANSWERS

1. C Georgia thought the bones she found in the desert were beautiful perfect shapes, and just the right color to include in her paintings.

2. a and c Georgia O'Keeffe played the violin and piano quite well. Music influenced many of her paintings. Georgia felt she could express a feeling of music through her arrangement of colors and shapes.

3. b and c Georgia always liked having cats around. She also once owned a large black French Poodle. She considered her Chow dogs, Bo and Chia, her best friends, though.

4. C Georgia preferred loose-fitting black dresses or long pants with simple white blouses. She wasn't interested in bling or fashion at all. Georgia wanted to be as comfortable as possible when she was tramping around the desert searching for interesting scenes to paint.

5. C Georgia was never crazy about snakes. While working on her mural-sized painting, she was always looking over her shoulder to make sure a rattlesnake from the desert hadn't snuck into the garage behind her.

HEY, WHAT DOES THAT WORD MEAN?

encourage (en-KUR-ij) To give someone confidence by praising or supporting him or her

gallery (GAL-uh-ree) A place where art is exhibited and sometimes sold

model (MOD-uhl) To pose for an artist

modern (MOD-urn) Describing the period of art from the late 1900s to the 1960s

original (uh-RIJ-uh-nuhl) New or unusual

rearrange (re-uh-RAYNJ) To arrange things differently

simplify (SIM-pluh-fye) To make something less complicated

talent (TAL-uhnt) Natural ability or skill

Visit this Scholastic Web site for more information on Georgia O'Keeffe:
www.factsfornow.scholastic.com
Enter the keyword **O'Keeffe**

INDEX